THE
FIDDLEHOPPERS

THE FIDDLEHOPPERS

CRICKETS, KATYDIDS, AND LOCUSTS

Phyllis J. Perry

A FIRST BOOK
FRANKLIN WATTS
A Division of Grolier Publishing
New York • London • Hong Kong • Sydney
Danbury, Connecticut

For Janet, my favorite fiddler,
and for Jill, who marches to
her own music.

Author's Note: "Fiddlehoppers" is not a scientific word.
It is a term I use to describe insects that make their music
by stridulating, or rubbing together two body parts.

Photographs copyright ©: Photo Researchers, Inc.: pp. 2 (N. Smythe/NAS),
8 (Nuridsany/Perennou), 16 (Stephen Dalton), 22 (J.H. Robinson),
24 (Stephen Dalton), 32 (Alvin E. Staffan/NAS), 40 (Gianni Tortoli),
45 (Nuridsany/Perennou), 52 (Rod Planck); Visuals Unlimited: pp. 11
(Kjell B. Sandved), 12 (Wm. S. Ormerod Jr.), 14 (Kjell B. Sandved),
19 (Joe McDonald), 28 (Tom Edwards), 34 (William M. Johnson),
36 (John D. Cunningham), 38 (Thomas Gula), 50; The Wildlife Collection:
pp. 20 (Charles Melton), 42 (Martin Harvey); Robert and Linda Mitchell:
pp. 27, 30; UPI/Bettmann: p. 46; The Bettmann Archive: p. 48;
Dwight Kuhn: p. 54; Steve Bourgeois: p. 56.

Library of Congress Cataloging-in-Publication Data

Perry, Phyllis Jean.
  The fiddlehoppers: crickets, katydids, and locusts / Phyllis J. Perry
    p. cm. — (A First book)
  Includes bibliographical references (p.   ) and index.
  Summary: Discusses crickets and grasshoppers, including katydids
and locusts, all insects that are known for their sounds and their hopping
abilities.
  ISBN 0-531-20209-7
  1. Orthoptera — Juvenile literature. 2. Grasshoppers — Juvenile literature.
3. Insect sounds — Juvenile literature. [1. Crickets. 2. Locusts. 3. Katydids.]
I. Title. II. Series.
QL506.P47 1995
595.7'26 — dc20   95-226
                                                       CIP AC

CONTENTS

THE
FIDDLEHOPPERS

These are the two small wings that a male cricket uses to make music. To chirp, he raises these wings and pulls the right wing over the left.

Chapter 1

THE MUSIC MAKERS

The real noisemakers of the insect world are the grasshoppers, including the katydids and locusts, and the crickets. These little creatures are not only tremendous hoppers, they are great fiddlers. The fiddlehoppers make their music by *stridulation,* which means that they make sound by rubbing together two body parts.

There are two main ways insects stridulate. One way used by crickets and field grasshoppers, such as katydids, is to rub their wings together. They have a file-and-scraper device on the underside of the two front wings. The file is a row of teethlike projections attached to a vein on the upper part of the left front wing. On

the upper edge of the right wing is the ridge that serves as a scraper.

When the cricket or katydid is at rest, the top of the left front wing overlaps the top of the right one. Then the two sound-making surfaces touch. By moving the wings, the insect chirps. This sound is magnified by a structure called a mirror, which is located near the file and scraper. The mirror is a circular section of wing membrane that is stretched tight, much like a drum. It picks up vibrations and amplifies them.

The second way insects, usually short-horned grasshoppers, stridulate is by rubbing their hind legs against their front wings. On the inside of the lower section of each hind leg there is a toothlike structure called the file. When this file is rubbed against a ridge of the front wing, much as a musician might pull a bow across a violin's strings, it sets up vibrations that are heard as sounds.

It is only the male fiddlehoppers that can make loud music, although females and young can make some sounds. The music-making mechanisms of the female are not as fully developed and prevent her from producing similar sounds. Some male insects can make sounds in the air, but they usually make their music at rest.

The music of the fiddlehoppers serves several purposes. The male fiddlehopper will use music for a mating call that brings the female to him. The female hears the male through *tympana*, which are like eardrums. Tympana vibrate as a result of sound waves, enabling an insect to pick up the sound that other insects of the same species make. Tympana are located in different spots, depending on the type of grasshopper. Some are found on the leg, some on the *thorax*, and some on the *abdomen*. On crickets, the eardrums are located just below the "knee joint" of the forelegs. Insects may also fiddle to warn of the approach of enemies.

Some of the fiddlehoppers make the same sound whenever they chirp. Others have different songs for different times of the day and night.

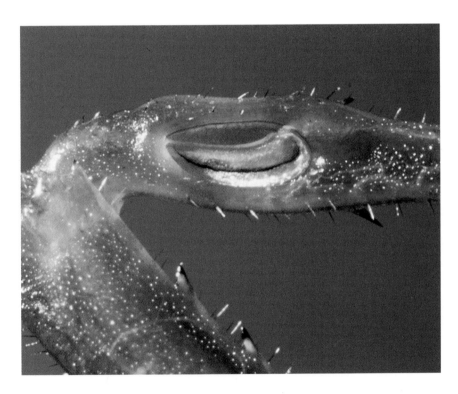

This katydid has a tympanum, or eardrum, on both sides of its leg.

This view of the underside of a grasshopper shows
its three body sections: the head, the thorax,
and the abdomen.

Chapter 2

MILLIONS OF INSECTS

There are almost a million different species of insects. In fact, insect species vastly outnumber all other kinds of animals combined. Although each species of insects is different, there are many ways in which all insects are alike. Like other insects, the fiddlehoppers need food and oxygen. They grow, move, and make more of their own kind.

All insect bodies have three parts: head, thorax, and abdomen. The head contains a tiny brain, nerves, eyes, *antennae,* and mouthparts. The thorax, or the middle section of the insect body, bears three pairs of legs and usually two pairs of wings. The abdomen contains organs for breathing, for digesting food, for mating, and in females, for egg laying.

The blood of an insect is usually either colorless, yellowish, or green, not at all like red human blood. When you slap and kill an insect, such as a mosquito, and see red blood, it is not the insect's blood that you are seeing. It is blood that the mosquito drew from some animal that it recently bit—usually that of the slapper!

An insect heart is also very different from a human one. The heart of an insect is a long tube of segments, which runs the whole length of the insect's body. Between

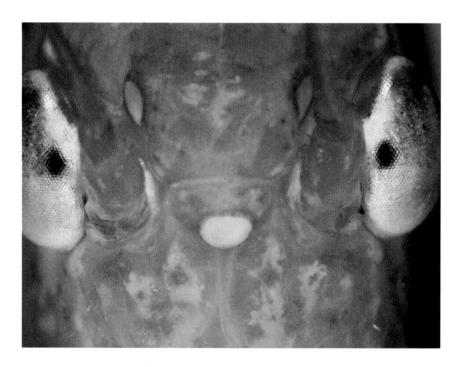

The grasshopper's two compound eyes bulge out to provide a wide field of vision; its other three eyes are in between.

the segments of the heart are valves. Some insects have tiny "hearts" at the bases of the antennae, legs, and wings that carry blood to these distant body parts.

Some insects have simple eyes, some have *compound eyes*, and some have a combination. The large compound eyes are really groups of little eyes.

Insects also have a nervous system that receives information about the outside world and controls the insect's body. An insect's nervous system is made up of a simple brain in the head, a main nerve cord that runs from the brain to the abdomen, messenger nerves, and *ganglia*. The ganglia are bunches of nerve cells along the nerve cord.

The straight-winged insects, which include crickets and grasshoppers, have narrow, long, and leathery front wings and wide hind wings. Both pairs of wings fold backward over the abdomen. A few of these insects have either tiny wings or none at all. Although the fiddle-hoppers have many characteristics in common, each group has its differences.

In proportion to its weight, a short-horned grasshopper, with its long, powerful hind legs, can outjump a kangaroo.

Chapter 3

GRASSHOPPERS

Grasshoppers and their relatives are large insects with chewing or biting mouthparts. They have two pairs of wings. The straight, front wings are thick and leathery. The hind wings are broad and filmy. When not in use, these flight wings are folded like a fan against the body and beneath the front wings.

Of all the fiddlehoppers, the grasshoppers are the best jumpers. They have large thigh muscles much like those of a frog. Grasshoppers can jump 3½ feet (about 1 m), a great distance considering their small size. A grasshopper can jump about twenty times its length and half that high.

When it jumps, the grasshopper usually jumps no farther than it can see so that it can pick out a safe landing spot. Because it is light, the grasshopper lands without harming its body. When a grasshopper is frightened, it may jump wildly.

A grasshopper can walk on all six of its legs. At the bottom of its feet are special pads that help the foot stick to a smooth surface. A grasshopper climbs by using the two claws at the end of each foot.

A grasshopper has five eyes. Two of its eyes are big compound eyes. These eyes are made up of hundreds of six-sided pieces, each of which is a small separate eye. The compound eyes are used to view objects several yards away. The three other eyes are very small and located between the two big compound eyes. One of the small eyes is in the middle of the face. The other two are found on the inside edge of each of the two big eyes. These three little eyes see only light and are used to view objects close to the grasshopper's face.

In spite of all their eyes, grasshoppers do not have especially good vision, because their eyes do not focus as human eyes do. Each facet in the compound eye receives a little image of the surroundings. All these little images put together make a whole. Since a moving object appears in one facet after another, the compound eyes are good at detecting movement.

A grasshopper smells with its antennae. The antennae are complicated sense organs. They have fine, tiny hairs that can detect if there are movements in the air and whether the air is dry or damp. Most of the bristles on the antennae, however, are organs of smell.

Grasshoppers have a complicated mouth that is well adapted for chewing. The mouth has something like a tongue, a pair of lips, and two pairs of jaws. The lips hold the food while the jaws with toothlike edges do most of the cutting and chewing.

Grasshoppers eat many things, including other insects, but their usual diet is grass, grain, and vegetables. They, in turn, are eaten by such creatures as birds, cats, frogs, toads, salamanders, snakes, and lizards. Skunks, foxes, ground squirrels, and mice also eat grasshoppers. There is one kind of grasshopper, however, that reverses the roles. Called the African mouse-catcher, it is so big it can eat very small mice!

A hungry lizard from the Galápagos Islands munches on a grasshopper.

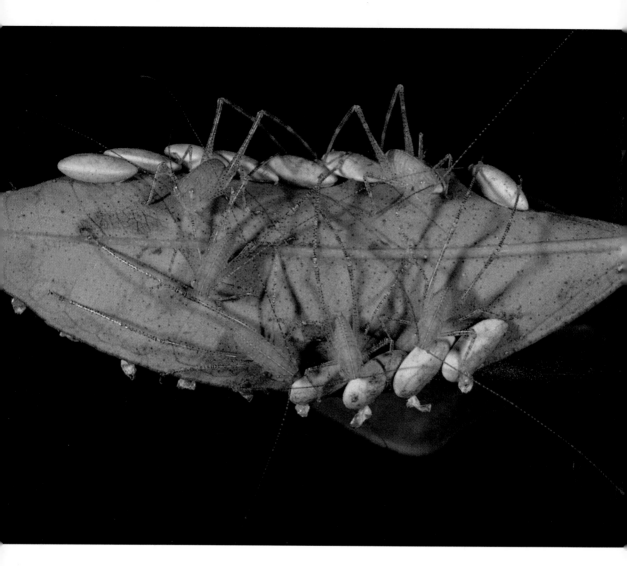

Katydid nymphs emerge from eggs the female laid on a leaf. The eggs overlap like roof shingles.

Although grasshoppers do not have lungs, they need oxygen to live. If you look very closely at a grasshopper, you can see some tiny spots on each side of its body. Each spot is a little breathing hole called a *spiracle*. Air comes in the breathing holes and goes through tiny tubes to every part of the grasshopper's body.

In the fall, most female grasshoppers deposit their eggs in a small hole in the ground or lay them on twigs, leaves, and stems. The eggs remain alive but dormant, or inactive, throughout the winter. From the egg comes a *nymph*, wrapped in a thin covering. Then the nymph crawls out of this covering and begins to eat and grow.

The young grasshopper looks like its parents, but it is much smaller and has no wings at first. As the nymph gets bigger, it molts, or sheds, its outer covering for a new coat. The new skin starts out soft but soon hardens. Before the outer skin is shed, a new one is formed underneath. A fluid between the two layers of skin helps to loosen the outer skin. To molt, the insect swallows air and blows itself up like a little balloon and splits its tight skin down the back. This process will occur about half a dozen times during the young grasshopper's growth period.

With the last molt, the wings are full grown. When these wings harden, the grasshopper is an adult. Sometimes, you can find the outgrown skins of a growing grasshopper outdoors.

Some people think that the grasshopper looks as if it is wearing armor. In fact, the grasshopper has an *exoskeleton*, or hard skin that covers its body.

**A grasshopper waits for its wings to dry
next to its recently molted skin.**

Grasshoppers, with their hard, smooth skin and joined body parts, resemble little machines. When a grasshopper flies, it uses both pairs of wings, although the hind wings do most of the work. A flying grasshopper looks like an airplane, with its upper wings held out much like the wings of a plane, while the hind wings work like propellers.

The grasshopper's hind legs may seem like a catapult, shooting the grasshopper into the air. Where the shins join the feet, a grasshopper's barbs look much like the spikes on the bottom of a sprinter's running shoe.

There are two kinds of grasshoppers: short-horned and long-horned. Grasshoppers don't really have horns but antennae. A short-horned grasshopper has short antennae; a long-horned grasshopper has long antennae. These two kinds of grasshoppers, some of which are also called locusts, have other differences beside the lengths of their antennae.

Grasshoppers fly by beating their wings up and down. The bigger hind wings produce more lift than the forewings.

Chapter 4

SHORT-HORNED GRASSHOPPERS

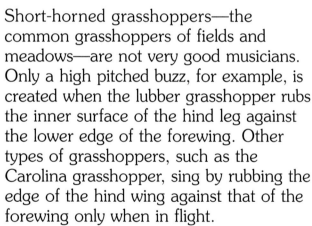

Short-horned grasshoppers—the common grasshoppers of fields and meadows—are not very good musicians. Only a high pitched buzz, for example, is created when the lubber grasshopper rubs the inner surface of the hind leg against the lower edge of the forewing. Other types of grasshoppers, such as the Carolina grasshopper, sing by rubbing the edge of the hind wing against that of the forewing only when in flight.

The short-horned grasshoppers feed on plants by using their scissorlike mouthparts, and they spit when disturbed. The brown juice, or what some people call "tobacco juice," that they spit out is partly digested grass.

There are many different kinds and colors of short-horned grasshoppers. The colors of grasshoppers tend to deepen as they grow older. One of the best known short-horned grasshoppers is the common red-legged grasshopper because its red legs make it stand out in its green surroundings.

In the United States, the biggest short-horned grasshoppers are the Carolina locusts. Their colors are brown, dull slate gray, reddish, or yellowish. Even though it looks drab sitting still, the Carolina locust has beautiful wings, especially when it spreads its black wings with their wide, pale yellow borders. A Carolina locust often rests on a dusty road or a bare patch of ground that resembles its dull coloring. Because of its modest coloring, this locust is sometimes called the Quaker, after a religious group known for simple, plain speech and clothing.

Another short-horned grasshopper, the clouded locust, is brown with spots. Some large locusts in Brazil have a special camouflage. Their wings are shaped and colored with patches to look like decaying or mildewed leaves—not very appetizing to hungry leaf-eating animals. On the other hand, some grasshoppers in the Galápagos Islands, off the coast of Ecuador, have strikingly bright colors, which may frighten off birds that otherwise might eat them.

One of the bulkiest of the grasshoppers is the lubber locust of the southeastern and southwestern United States. These insects have very stubby wings and great, heavy bodies. They feed on plants, and their chief enemy is the sparrow hawk.

These eastern lubber grasshoppers are more colorful than the western ones.

One of the smallest kinds of grasshoppers is the pygmy locust, which measures less than ½ inch (about 1 cm) long. Unlike most grasshoppers, the pygmy locusts, which are found in the southern part of the United States, survive through the winter. After the first thaw, you can see them crawling out from under the bark of a tree to sun themselves.

A few of the band-winged southern locusts also survive winter. Instead of hatching in the spring, they hatch in the middle of the summer. By fall, they have not yet made their final molt. When the weather turns cold, these locusts crawl under bits of bark or clumps of dirt and sleep through the winter. Then in May, they molt again and get their wings.

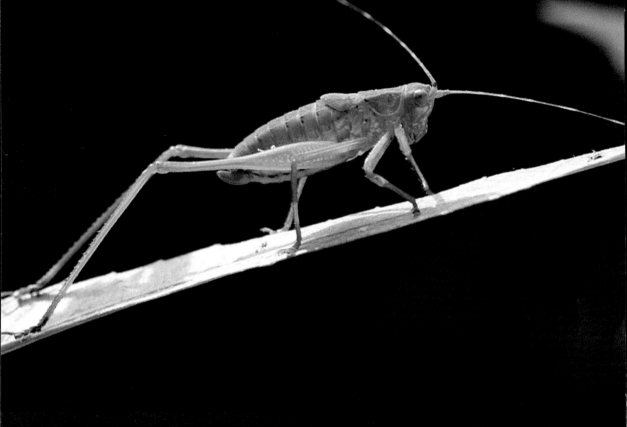

Long-horned grasshoppers have long, threadlike
antennae. This one is a fork-tailed bush katydid.

Chapter 5

LONG-HORNED GRASSHOPPERS

The long-horned grasshoppers are called katydids. They are about 2 inches (5 cm) long, but their long, thin antennae are often longer than their bodies. Katydids are usually a bright green, but on rare occasions are bright pink.

There are many different kinds of katydids, including the large, oblong-winged tree katydid, the fork-tailed bush katydid, the conehead katydid from the field, cave katydids, and the common meadow katydid. Some katydids live in and eat the leaves of cherry, apple, oak, or maple trees. Others live in grass.

The male katydids make their music by raising and rubbing their front wings quickly back and forth. One wing has teeth, the other has a kind of scraper located where the wings overlap. Each kind of katydid has its own song. Frequently heard on summer nights, the katydid call can come as often as once a second. Katydids seldom make a sound when the temperature is below 60°F (16°C).

A group of katydids can be noisy. These fiddlehoppers get their name from the noise that the leaf-winged katydid makes when it is singing at night, which sounds like

The female katydid lays her eggs early in the fall with her long, swordlike ovipositor.

someone saying "Katy did" and then "Katy didn't!" In the South, they are sometimes called Cackle-Jacks.

When it is time to lay eggs, the female katydid lays between 100 and 150. The eggs are laid in the fall and hatch in the spring. Tree, bush, and meadow katydids lay their eggs on the plants they eat such as meadow grasses, tree bark, and edges of leaves and twigs.

The bush katydid lays eggs that are very flat. When she is ready to deposit her eggs, she first bites away the rim of the leaf. Then, using her egg-placer, she places her flat eggs between the upper and lower layers of a single leaf. In time, the leaf heals over the little bulges of the eggs.

Cave katydids use their egg-placers to dig a hole in the dirt and plant their slender eggs in the ground. A new hole is dug for each egg.

There are three kinds of long-horned grasshoppers that are often mistaken for crickets: the Mormon cricket, the sand cricket, and the camel or cave cricket. A Mormon cricket is a large, black, wingless grasshopper found in the high mountains of the western United States.

In years when Mormon crickets are especially abundant, they can cause great damage. They eat sugar beets and the seed heads of wheat and do the most damage to cattle and sheep grazing lands. Because they especially enjoy flower and seed parts, the Mormon crickets may prevent grasses that livestock feed on from reseeding themselves.

The sand cricket is a wingless grasshopper that lives on the sandy soil of the West Coast. Camel crickets or cave crickets have a short-humpbacked body and stout hind legs. They live in caves, hollow logs, and dark, moist places.

Like some grasshoppers, crickets have long antennae.
Unlike all grasshoppers, a cricket's wing covers
lie flat on its back.

Chapter 6

CRICKETS

Crickets and grasshoppers belong to the orthopteran order of insects. Crickets have a shiny black head and a black or blackish-brown body. A male cricket is about 1 inch (2½ cm) long. Females may be still bigger.

It is easy to tell a cricket from a grasshopper by looking carefully at its wings. The wing covers of grasshoppers meet at a peak and the wings lie at rest on a slope. The wing covers of a cricket lie flat on the back and fold down on the sides like a tablecloth covering a picnic table.

A cricket has jointed antennae, which are covered with thousands of tiny bristles. These detect the movement of air and also tell whether the air is dry or

**Although many crickets are black, some, such as
this snowy tree cricket, are lighter colored.**

damp. Some of the bristles pick up sounds, but most of these bristles and pegs on the antennae are organs of smell.

The cricket also has very fine hairs on its body and on its rear *cerci*, or feelers. These hairs respond to air and sound waves. If you try to grab a cricket from behind, the cricket will feel the air currents and can jump away to a safer place. The cricket uses its mouth to clean these sensitive hairs.

Some insects eat animals and others eat vegetables. House crickets have a mouth that will let them eat both kinds of food. The mouth is a hole at the front of the head. The opening is surrounded by mouthparts. There is a flat upper lip and a lower lip. Two biting jaws open and close sideways and cut food into small pieces. Behind these, a smaller pair of jaws passes the food into the cricket's mouth.

Crickets make many different kinds of noises depending on the type of insect and the outdoor temperature. The warmer it is, the faster crickets chirp. They seldom chirp when the temperature rises over 100°F (38°C) or below 55°F (13°C).

The snowy tree cricket or "thermometer cricket" gets its name because the warmer the weather, the faster it chirps. The tempo of the chirping is so closely linked to the temperature that you can guess the temperature by carrying out a simple math problem. Add forty to the number of chirps a cricket makes in fifteen seconds, and you get a close approximation of the actual air temperature in Fahrenheit. These crickets are not only

**Before she lays eggs, the tree cricket punctures
a plant stem. These holes are the nests into which
she drops her eggs, shown here.**

helpful thermometers, they also eat plant lice and other insect pests.

All of a cricket's six feet have claws that let them cling to rocks and even move across ceilings. A cricket also has two sharp spikes that stick out from its back. These spikes help the cricket move backward. The female has an extra spike in back that her eggs slide down as she is putting them in the ground.

Crickets molt like grasshoppers. As the young cricket grows, a new skin forms under the old one. A chemical helps weaken the old skin. The outer layer finally splits apart and the cricket steps out in its new, white skin. In a few hours, the soft skin hardens and grows darker. A young cricket will molt eight to ten times before becoming an adult. Its wings appear after the sixth or seventh molt.

Like short-horned grasshoppers, crickets make music by drawing a special vein on the underside of the right wing over a rough spot on the surface of the left wing. The special vein has more than a hundred tiny ridges on it. The male cricket raises its wings at a 45-degree angle to its body and moves them across each other, much like opening and closing a pair of scissors. The wings and body form an echo chamber that makes the chirps louder.

A field cricket, like most crickets, has an eardrum near the knee of each front leg. In addition to large compound eyes, field crickets have three tiny single eyes. These are in the middle of its face between the large, compound eyes. Field crickets also make holes in the ground where they lay their eggs.

Near the mouth are two pairs of *palps* that are used somewhat like people use hands. When a cricket chews, the jaws move sideways. Crickets will eat plants, soft-bodied insects, and even fibers in clothing.

The ground cricket is much smaller than the field cricket and moves with giant leaps. His music is a faint trill. The male ground cricket is blackish brown; the larger female has dark stripes across the lighter brown abdomen.

The largest kind of cricket, the mole cricket, spends most of its life underground or under rocks in damp places. The mole cricket prefers to live in moist soil near

The destructive mole cricket eats the roots of lawn grasses and uproots seedlings as it burrows.

swamps and ponds. This cricket eats roots and seedlings, often ruining popular commercial plants such as strawberry and peanut plants. Because of its hard, shell-like body, it is sometimes called an earth crab.

Usually underground, the mole cricket does little leaping. Its front legs are thick and sturdy and good for digging. Its forewings are short. Above ground, the mole cricket can fly with his long wings and chirp using the upper pad. Like a moth, this cricket sometimes flies to electric lights.

Many crickets lay their eggs in damp sand by depositing them through the egg-laying tube. When the female mole cricket lays eggs, she first hollows out a nest and tunnels a network of connecting passageways. She lays her eggs and then guards them, waiting for any enemy in the tunnels. The male mole cricket will eat its young if he gets the chance.

Helped by rising warm air, these migratory grasshoppers in Ethiopia glitter as they fly high in the sky.

Chapter 7

LOCUSTS

Because some insects do a lot of harm, we often consider them enemies. One group of fiddlehoppers, the locust, is among the most destructive of insects. Locusts are short-horned grasshoppers that come in two forms or "phases"—a solitary phase and a gregarious phase. The solitary locusts like to be alone, but the gregarious locusts travel in huge swarms.

Locusts live in dry places, but the female must lay her eggs in wet soil. When the young locusts hatch, they tunnel up through the soil to the sunlight and begin feeding on plants. If there are so many hoppers in one area that the food runs out, these hoppers may grow into the "swarming" type of locust.

**These locusts are mating. Like most grasshoppers,
the male is smaller than the female.**

When hoppers grow up where there is plenty of food, they do not swarm but grow into "solitary" locusts. They migrate on their own, instead of in a swarm, and fly high in the sky at night. Within its lifetime of a few weeks, the solitary locust may migrate 60 miles (96 km).

Sometimes when conditions, such as visual stimulation, temperature, humidity, and availability of food, are just right, the *prothoracic gland* in the grasshopper *secretes* hormones that cause the solitary insect to change to a swarming, migratory insect. The members of these swarms are called locusts.

Some swarms travel as far as 2,000 miles (3,220 km) in their search for food and damp places to lay their eggs. These swarming locusts grow, turn colors, and change their mating and feeding habits. And they grow longer wings that let them fly great distances.

Swarms of "gregarious" grasshoppers can destroy a tremendous number of crops. It is estimated that as many as several billion of these insects may swarm together, making a flying, living "cloud" 1 mile (1.6 km) wide, 100 feet deep (30 m) deep, and over 50 miles (80 km) long. Swarms of locusts usually travel by day and follow the winds. The strong, heavily veined wings of locusts let them travel 60 to 70 miles (about 97 to 113 km) a day.

Swarms of locusts appear most frequently in Africa, South America, and the Near East. One 1958 swarm in Somalia contained an estimated 40 billion locusts, capable of eating 80,000 tons of food a day. There have also been swarms in India, Russia, southern Europe, and Central America.

North America has seen many locust swarms over the years. In 1740, when millions of insects attacked crops in the Massachusetts Bay Colony, the early American settlers used homemade brush brooms to sweep the insects into the ocean.

The most famous swarm in the United States appeared in Utah in 1848. Locusts threatened to destroy the frontier settlement of Brigham Young, a leader of the Mormon Church. This ferocious locust swarm could have put an end to the new town. Just in time, flocks of seagulls flew in, ate the swarm of locusts, and saved the settlement. The seagull was made Utah's state bird and the subject of a well-known monument in Salt Lake City, Utah.

In the 1870s, the Rocky Mountain region had such massive swarms of grasshoppers, they affected train schedules. The bodies of the grasshoppers were so thick on the train tracks that the engine wheels spun on the tracks and skidded past stations.

In 1874, millions of locusts destroyed corn and wheat fields in Kansas. For the next three years, locusts swarmed from Texas to the Dakotas and from the Rocky Mountains to the Mississippi River. By 1878, these locusts had almost vanished. No Rocky Mountain locusts have been seen in the United States since the turn of the century. This particular species may be extinct, but no one knows for certain.

During the 1930s, locusts swarmed again in the United States. This time they hit during a drought that turned the Great Plains into what was called the "Dust Bowl." Warm temperatures and scarcity of food where the young hoppers were growing up caused them to swarm.

Two desert locusts devour a leaf. When large numbers
of these insects are feeding, they can ruin entire crops.

An abundance of grasshoppers, a lack of plants and grasses, and warm air can cause swarming. The last swarm in America like this was in the 1930s.

Since the Dust Bowl, swarms of locusts have not been seen in North America. And very large swarms of locusts have not been seen in Africa since the 1960s. Many of these locusts have been killed by insecticides.

Locust swarms have caused much damage over the years and scientists are working hard to develop chemicals to control them. Finding a way to prevent the prothoracic gland from functioning, for example, would prevent the solitary grasshopper from turning into a migratory swarming locust.

The United Nations Food and Agriculture Organization has even organized international efforts in locust control. When swarms of locusts, called a plague, sweep into an area, teams of technicians work to fight the swarms, spraying them with an atomized mist from aircraft.

It is difficult, however, to find a chemical that will work on pests without injuring humans or other animals. Some insecticides that enter the food chain and harm various animals have been banned in the United States.

**Many books and illustrations, such as this one,
have described how frontier plagues devastated
precious crops and hopes.**

Chapter 8

FIDDLEHOPPERS IN FICTION AND HISTORY

Grasshoppers and crickets have had some very interesting stories written about them. The most famous is Aesop's fable about the ant and the grasshopper. This story illustrates the value of hard work. In this tale, the ant stores up food for winter and never stops to play. Meanwhile, the grasshopper fiddles away the summer months. When the cold weather comes, it is the industrious ant that is ready.

In modern times, the story of Pinocchio, a living puppet whose nose grows when he tells a lie, features a cricket. In another all-time favorite, *The Cricket in Times Square* by George Selden, a cricket falls asleep in a picnic basket in a Connecticut meadow and awakes in a New York City subway station. A popular children's picture book called *The Very Quiet Cricket* by Eric Carle is about a young cricket who finally achieves his wish to make music.

Several children's books describe the massive, destructive grasshopper plagues of the frontier during the 1800s. In *Grasshopper Summer* by Ann Turner, a swarm

Locust swarms have caused problems since ancient times. This ancient Egyptian tablet shows a grasshopper eating crops.

of locusts threatens the survival of a young boy and his family. In *On the Banks of Plum Creek,* Laura Ingalls Wilder shares her family's adventures traveling by covered wagon to Minnesota and the grasshopper plague that destroys their wheat fields.

Grasshopper plagues have been seen all over the world for a long time. Records of locust swarms can be found in the Bible, in ancient Aztec art, in decorations on ancient Egyptian tombs, and in Chinese literature.

In ancient China, crickets, thought to bring good luck, were often kept as pets in beautiful cages and special containers. Some were kept for the music they made, and others because they were great fighters. People were proud of their pet crickets and took good care of them. Some people would take their pet crickets to picnics and hang the cages in trees and listen to the crickets sing.

Many people in China held cricket fights and bet large amounts of money on their favorite cricket champion. Fighters were weighed in on tiny scales and matched with an opponent of equal size. To get them to fight, a hair tickler was used to excite the crickets. These cricket fights are the topic of several books, including Alison Stilwell's *Chin Ling, the Chinese Cricket* and Feenie Ziner's *Cricket Boy: A Chinese Tale.*

Cricket fights were also common in the Dutch East Indies. Two crickets would meet in front of their bamboo boxes. The first one to push the other back into its box won the fight. These crickets seldom hurt each other.

Young grasshoppers, or nymphs—such as this one—
have not developed wings to fly away with,
so you might find them easy to catch.

Chapter 9

SOME ACTIVITIES TO LEARN MORE

Photography

One way to learn more about fiddlehoppers is to capture them on film in their natural surroundings. First you will need to find a place where fiddlehoppers are plentiful, perhaps in a park, dry field, or vacant lot. Then, you will need a camera.

You have to use a high speed film (at least ISO 400) and a fast shutter speed ($\frac{1}{500}$ or $\frac{1}{1,000}$ of a second) or your pictures will turn out blurry if you move or the fiddlehopper jumps. Taking your pictures in well-lit areas will also help your photos come out focused.

Keep a notebook to record the date, time, and place, as well as the lighting conditions, film, and shutter speeds.

To protect themselves, grasshoppers jump and fly
away. It is easier to catch them with a net
attached to a long pole.

Measuring the Big Jump

Grasshoppers and crickets have very large thigh muscles. When these thigh muscles tighten, they pull back on the knee joints, which causes the lower legs to swing back. Since the feet are anchored to the ground, the force of the muscles pushes the insect's body up and forward.

You can find out for yourself just how far grasshoppers jump. Record your own guess. Then, you will need to catch a grasshopper. Try using a butterfly net or a net from a fish aquarium.

Once you have caught a grasshopper, you can keep it for a short time in a clean, empty jar with air holes punctured in the lid.

To carry out your test, set out a long sheet of paper and mark a starting point with a pen. Place the grasshopper at the starting point and make it jump by touching its tail with a feather. Mark another point where the grasshopper lands and measure the distance from the starting point. Try it with several grasshoppers, and crickets, too, and see if your guess was close. When you are finished with your experiment, return the insects to the area where you captured them.

Record your data in your notebook.

Keeping Crickets as Pets

Crickets make good pets at home or at school. You can assemble a home for a cricket by putting a layer of soil and some leaves into an empty aquarium with a wire mesh top. Sprinkle some water on the leaves or put a small bottle cap of water in the cage for the cricket to

**After studying and enjoying a fiddlehopper,
be sure to release it outside.**

drink. Put your cricket into this new habitat and you will have a *vivarium*.

If you keep more than one cricket, you need to be sure that you have a male and female, because two males or two females will often fight. You can identify the female cricket from the long spike on her abdomen. Remember females do not chirp, so if you want a pet cricket to make music for you, you will have to catch a male cricket.

If you do decide to keep a pet cricket, you will need to keep its cage clean and feed it. Pet crickets will eat bits of ordinary food—crumbs of bread, raisins, lettuce, cucumbers, potatoes, and even dog biscuits. Crickets need only a small amount of food. If you give proper care, you can enjoy your pet fiddlehopper for a long time.

GLOSSARY

Abdomen — The third, rear section of an insect's body.

Antennae — A pair of movable jointed sensory organs located on an insect's head.

Cerci — A pair of feelers at the end of an insect's body that usually act as sensory organs.

Compound eye — The large eye of an insect made up of many smaller lenses.

Exoskeleton — The hard "skin" of arthropoda, a classification that includes the grasshoppers.

Ganglia — Masses of nerve cells that function as nerve centers.

Nymph — The middle, immature stage of an insect that goes through several changes in form.

Palps — Fingerlike insect mouthparts that touch or taste.

Prothoracic gland — The gland that controls the change from a solitary locust to a migratory locust.

Secrete — To produce and give off a liquid or substance.

Spiracle — One of the tiny breathing holes on the sides of an insect's body.

Stridulation — The production of shrill noises by male insects by rubbing together two body parts.

Thorax — The middle section of an insect's body where wings and legs are attached.

Tympana — An insect's eardrums.

Vivarium — A container for keeping or raising small animals, such as crickets, indoors.

FOR FURTHER READING

Ames, Lee J. *Draw 50 Creepy Crawlers.* New York: Doubleday, 1991.

Bailey, Jill. *The Life Cycle of a Grasshopper.* New York: Bookwright, 1990.

Greenbacker, Liz. *Bugs: Stingers, Suckers, Sweeties, Swingers.* New York: Franklin Watts, 1993.

Johnson, Sylvia A. *Chirping Insects.* Minneapolis: Lerner Publications, 1986.

Mound, Laurence Alfred. *Amazing Insects.* New York: Alfred A. Knopf, 1993.

Oram, Liz, and R. Robin Baker. *Insect Migration.* Austin, Tex.: Raintree Steck-Vaughn, 1992.

Parker, Steve. *Insects.* New York: Dorling Kindersley, 1992.

Snedden, Robert. *What Is an Insect?* San Francisco: Sierra Club Books for Children, 1993.

Suzuki, David T. *Looking at Insects.* New York: Wiley, 1992.

INDEX

ABOUT
THE AUTHOR

Phyllis J. Perry has worked as an elementary school teacher and principal and has written two dozen books for teachers and young people. She received her doctorate in Curriculum and Instruction from the University of Colorado, where she currently supervises student teachers. Dr. Perry lives with her husband, David, in Boulder, Colorado.